Once upon a time, in a small town called Harmonyville, there lived three cousins: Aurora, Cade, and Conor.

They loved spending their summer days together, exploring the beautiful beach that was just a short walk from their homes.

One sunny morning, as the cousins set off to the beach, they noticed a small crab scuttling across the sand.

Aurora, the oldest and wisest of the three, gently picked it up and showed it to her younger brother Cade and cousin Conor.

They were fascinated by its tiny claws and colorful shell.

As they continued their walk along the shore, they came upon a group of children building sandcastles.

They watched with excitement as the children laughed and played.

But suddenly, one of the children accidentally knocked down another child's sandcastle.

The child who built the sandcastle became very angry
and started shouting.

Aurora, Cade, and Conor looked at each other, unsure of what to do.

Aurora remembered the lessons their parents had taught them about anger and how it can be both a good and a bad emotion.

She decided it was the perfect opportunity to teach her younger brother and cousin about the concept of anger.

She explained to them that anger is a natural emotion that everyone feels from time to time, just like being happy or sad.

She told them that anger can be a good thing because it gives us energy to protect ourselves or others, or to take action against something that is wrong.

But she also emphasized that it's important to control our anger and use it in a positive way.

Aurora shared a story from the Bible about Jesus and how he handled his anger.

She told them about the time Jesus went to the temple and saw people buying and selling instead of praying and worshiping.

Jesus became angry because he knew it was wrong to disrespect God's house.

But instead of lashing out in anger, he used his anger to teach others an important lesson about what was right.

Anger

Anger is a God given emotion that gives us energy to protect ourselves, someone else, or to take action against something that is happening that is wrong.

Anger is just another emotion we have just like being happy or sad.

It is not a bad emotion.

It can often protect us or the people we love.

Jesus even taught us anger is not a bad emotion.

Anger is what happens to us when we are threatened, offended, wronged, or denied something we really want or need.

What we do with our anger can sometimes be bad though.

Aurora encouraged Cade and Conor to think about how they could use their anger in a positive way, just like Jesus did.

She suggested that instead of getting angry and shouting when something goes wrong, they could calmly express their feelings and try to find a solution.

Jesus taught us how to deal with anger.

He taught us to:

1) Understand Why we are Angry
2) Deal with it Immediately
3) Deal with our Anger in a Controlled manner
4) Teach others why we are Angry
5) Show Compassion

The cousins continued their walk along the beach, now with a deeper understanding of anger.

They promised each other that they would always try to use their anger in a positive way, just like Jesus did.

They knew that with their newfound knowledge, they could make a difference in the world and help others understand the importance of handling anger with love and compassion.

And so, as the sun set over the horizon, the three cousins walked hand in hand, ready to face any challenges that came their way, armed with the wisdom of how to use their anger for good.

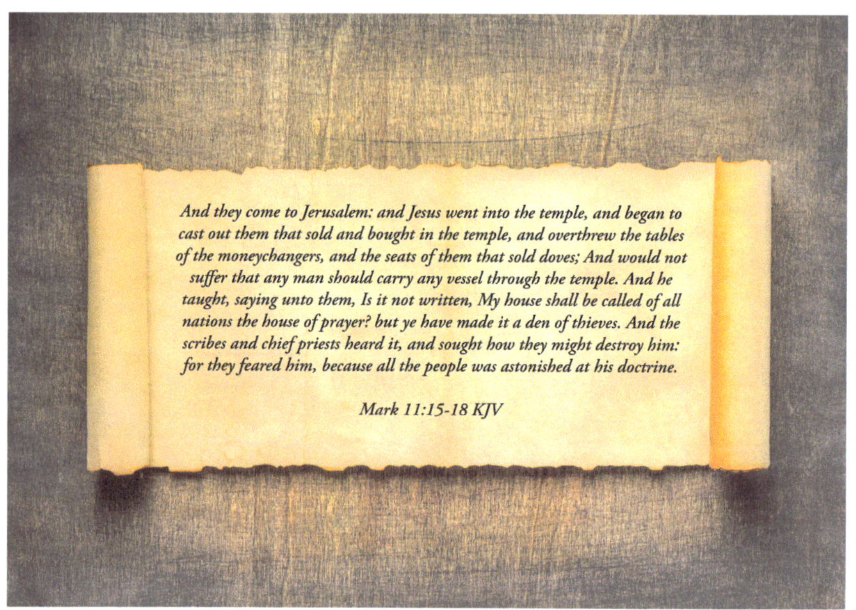
And they come to Jerusalem: and Jesus went into the temple, and began to
cast out them that sold and bought in the temple, and overthrew the tables
of the moneychangers, and the seats of them that sold doves; And would not
suffer that any man should carry any vessel through the temple. And he
taught, saying unto them, Is it not written, My house shall be called of all
nations the house of prayer? but ye have made it a den of thieves. And the
scribes and chief priests heard it, and sought how they might destroy him:
for they feared him, because all the people was astonished at his doctrine.

Mark 11:15-18 KJV

About the Author

Lady Kimberly Motes Doty has dedicated her life to helping people in many different ways.

She is a minister, which means she helps others find their spiritual path.

She is also a life coach, which means she guides people to live their best lives.

Lady Kimberly is even a natural health specialist, which means she knows a lot about taking care of our bodies and staying healthy.

In addition to all of this, she loves to write and share her wisdom with others.

When she's not working, she enjoys spending time with her family.

https://ladykimberlyindustries.godaddysites.com/

https://mybook.to/LadyKimberlyBooks

More Lady Kimberly Children's Books

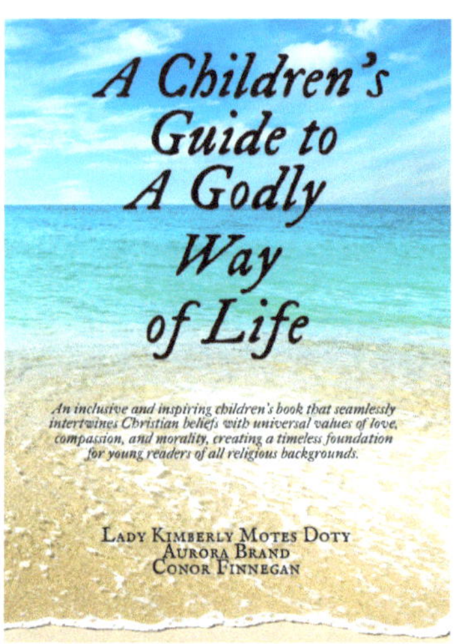

Introducing children to the wonders of God and the teachings of the Bible is a vital aspect of their spiritual development. That's why "A Children's Guide to A Godly Way of Life" is the ideal resource to nurture their curiosity and guide them towards a deeper understanding of faith. By introducing them to the commandments and the valuable lessons Jesus taught us about living a godly life, we can provide them with a solid foundation in their spiritual journey.

"A Children's Guide to a Godly Way of Life" is not just another ordinary book. It is a treasure trove of knowledge and wonder, carefully crafted to quench the thirst for understanding that resides within every child's soul. With each turn of the page, their imagination will ignite, propelling them on a lifelong voyage of love and devotion to God, and an insatiable hunger for unraveling the mysteries of the divine.

"Discovering God's Love: A Magical Journey of Faith and Wonder"

Introducing a captivating new children's book series by the talented author, Lady Kimberly Motes Doty. "Discovering God's Love" is an exploration of God's love and teachings through enchanting and relatable stories that conveys the sense of curiosity and discovery that young readers will experience as they delve into each book. "Discovering God's Love" emphasizes the spiritual growth and lifelong connection with God. The first five books in the series have been released with the full series to include short stories about the commandments, how to treat others, how to treat animals, and our own personal growth with God.

This extraordinary collection aims to teach children about God's boundless love and His teachings from the Bible through enchanting short stories. Lady Doty has masterfully crafted these tales to speak directly to children in a language they can easily understand, making each book both Biblically based and effortlessly relatable.

"What is God?" is a captivating children's book that follows the curious and kind-hearted girl, Aurora, on a quest to uncover the answer to a timeless question: What or who is God?

"Where is God?" is a heartwarming children's book that follows the journey of Aurora, a curious young girl, as she seeks to understand the presence of God. Wondering where God is, Aurora embarks on a quest to discover His whereabouts.

"Does God Lie?" is a touching tale that follows the journey of two siblings, Aurora and Cade, as they stumble upon a mysterious old book about God's promises. Intrigued by the idea of unwavering faithfulness, they embark on a quest to learn more about the reliability of God's word.

Join Aurora, Cade, and Conor on a thrilling treasure hunt that takes them on a journey through the wonders of God's creation in "Is Everything God Does Good?" This encouraging story reminds young readers of the beauty and love found in God's creations and the importance of being good stewards of the natural world.

"What Are Angels?" is a uplifting children's book that explores the concept of angels and their role in our lives. Through the eyes of a curious little boy named Cade, author Lady Kimberly Motes Doty takes young readers on a journey of discovery and understanding. Cade's fascination with angels leads him to ask his mother about their purpose and how they keep us safe. In response, his loving mother imparts wisdom and shares stories from the Bible. She explains angels, although invisible to the human eye, are like superheroes sent by God to watch over and protect us.

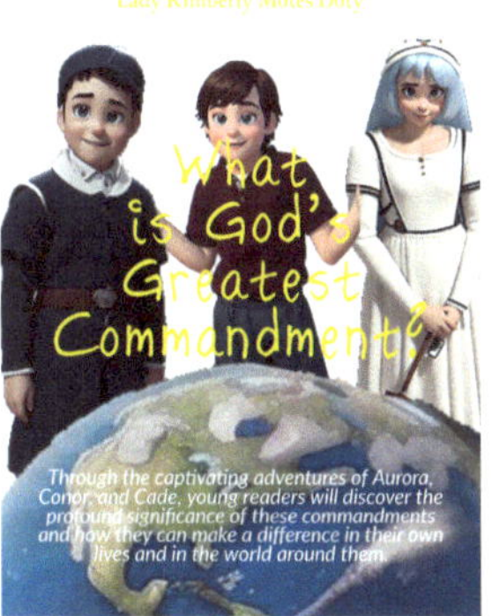

The uplifting children's book, "What is God's Greatest Commandment?" takes readers on another journey with the three curious and compassionate cousins Aurora, Conor, and Cade. One day, while playing near a majestic oak tree, they happen upon a special book called the Bible. As they open its pages, they discover the concept of commandments - rules given by God to guide them in living a purposeful and fulfilling life. Driven by their newfound understanding, Aurora, Conor, and Cade embark on a mission to put these commandments into action in their daily lives.

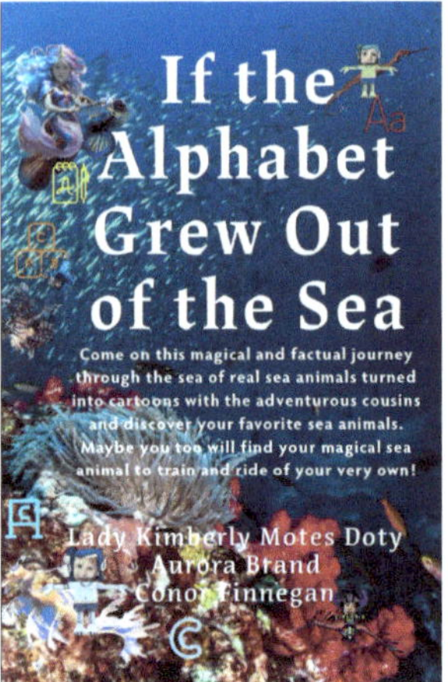

"If The Alphabet Grew Out of The Sea v2" - Almost 600 pages of mazes, word searches and fun facts about sea animals on an exciting Sea Adventure!

"If the Alphabet Grew Out of The Sea" V1 - in English, French & Spanish